THE CAREER EDGE
TAKE THE NEXT STEP
MASTER THE SKILLS THAT WILL SET YOU APART

BY LUCAS VITELLO

About the Author

Even as a child, I was developing my understanding of what a strong work ethic looked like. I was fortunate to have two capable and hardworking parents who modeled that every single day. Sometimes, I'd even join my dad on side jobs, where I got to apply the values they were teaching me firsthand.

I started working a formal job as soon as I was able to get my working papers. I held many jobs over the years, but it wasn't until I turned 17 that I began to understand the difference between simply having a job and engaging in work that could serve as a catalyst for a career. At the time, I was employed at a big-box retailer, where I met my first mentor—Dave, the store manager. I had inherited a strong work ethic from my parents, but I lacked direction. Dave changed that. He took me under his wing and showed me how to think beyond my current role and start seeing the big picture.

I had an interest in technology, and Dave encouraged me to lean into that curiosity. He created opportunities for me to apply what I was learning, challenged me to grow, and pushed me to excel. Under his mentorship, I became one of the company's top sales reps in technology and a subject matter expert in tech troubleshooting. But Dave's lessons extended beyond my department. He taught me not to view the store as a collection of isolated departments, but as pieces of a larger whole. I learned about departments beyond my own, studied store financials and business processes, and gained insights into the employees, their roles, and the different types of customers we served.

You might be wondering why I'm telling you about a job I had at 17—but that job, and more importantly the lessons I learned there, laid the foundation for everything that came after. Those fundamentals have guided my path ever since.

Over the years, I've built on that early foundation with every new experience. It's led me to successfully launch and run my own company, consult with other businesses on finding their path to success, and build a rewarding career at a Fortune 100 company. I started in an entry-level role, but by using the skills I share in this book, I grew my career year after year to where I am today, a Lead role in IT, and a Subject Matter Expert for the entire company.

I believe it's important that you, as the reader, know a little about who I am. But let me be clear—this isn't a book about me. This is a book for you. My story isn't what made me successful; it's what I learned along the way that gave me my edge. Now, I'm passing those lessons on to you—so you can make them part of your own journey.

CONTENTS

INTRODUCTION

Making it in your career isn't about talent, luck, or being in the right place at the right time, but your mindset, your habits, and your readiness. Train yourself for success—this book will help you build a strong foundation for your career by focusing on principles that will help you in the long run.

Too many people chase promotions, pay raises, or titles without first mastering the fundamentals. Career progress is earned long before you ever even see it: by learning continuously, doing everything you take on with excellence, cultivating solid relationships, and setting up for those opportunities ahead of time. These principles do more than help you climb the career ladder; they also make you more valuable in whatever role, industry, or situation you find yourself in.

In the chapters that follow, we'll cover key career principles that have supported people in a variety of industries achieve success. You'll find out how to create a continuous learning mindset, commit to little things with same conviction as the big things, communicate effectively, and be better prepared for opportunities. Whether you are just getting started or eager to progress in your career, these lessons will give you an edge and help you flourish.

How to Use This Book

Every chapter revolves around a core career theme, sharing insights, real-world examples and concrete action points. As you read, I challenge you to think about how those concepts tie into your own career and make an honest effort to put them into practice in your daily job.

It is time to take ownership of your career — are you ready? Let's dive in.

CHAPTER 1:

LEARN HOW TO LEARN

Success in any profession isn't necessarily about what you know — it's about how quickly and effectively you are able to learn new things. The best professionals are not the ones who have all the answers — they're the ones who know how to find them. The most valuable skill you can acquire in an ever-changing world with a fast-evolving job market driven by technological advancement is to learn how to learn.

THE POWER OF A GROWTH MINDSET

Your mindset is one of the biggest considerations when it comes to your learning. Psychologist Dr. Carol Dweck developed the growth mindset, which is defined as believing that effort and practice can develop abilities and intelligence. Having a growth mindset means seeing challenges as opportunities to strengthen and grow rather than obstacles to overcome.

This contrasts with a fixed mindset where individuals believe their skills and intelligence are more ridged. People with fixed mindset avoid and try to run from challenges for fear of failing. But in fact, failure is one of the best teachers. Each error is a chance for you to enhance your methods and improve. Having a growth mindset means making the investment in yourself to learn throughout your career, continual learning is key to your career success.

Another talent that develops with a growth mindset is resilience. When you believe growth is possible, failure is a temporary hurdle instead of a dead end. It is the willingness to take risks, the ability to leave your comfort zone and persevere. The secret is to replace the thought "I'm not good at this" with "I'm not good at this yet." That one word — yet — opens up room for learning and growth.

Regular exposure to new challenges is also the best way to grow a growth mindset. And it's because when you put yourself in a position outside of your expertise, you're putting yourself in a learning position, and that is how you train yourself to learn. Every new undertaking — whether it's a new skill required for work, a foreign language or a new hobby that requires patience and persistence — builds and hones your capacity for effective learning.

OVERCOMING FEAR OF FAILURE

Fear of failure is one of the main causes of the lack of the learning habit. Because they fear making mistakes, looking incompetent and failing in public, many professionals are holding themselves back. Failure is an essential aspect of learning and should be welcomed rather than shy away from. The most successful people in every field have failed many times before reaching success.

For instance, over 1,000 times Thomas Edison failed at creating the light bulb. When reflecting on his many failures, he turned his perspective, and stated, "I have not failed. I've just discovered 10,000 ways that won't work." It is this mentality of looking at failure as feedback, not a personal flaw, that enables people to carry on and progress.

To combat the fear of failure, a good exercise is to think about situations in the past where you failed, and how that ultimately lead you to a better situation. Because we all have that experience where something didn't go the way we wanted it to, but it taught us something that ultimately changed us or re-routed us to something better. Once you change your view on failure you see that it is a part of the learning process.

Learn by Doing – Passive learning, which takes the form of reading or watching a video, has its place, but through taking action and actually doing, this is the optimal way to learn. If you're learning a new software, play around with it. If you're learning a new skill, use it in your work. Learning by doing challenges you to understand concepts in a way that reading or watching a video simply can not.

Imagine if you're learning how to give a good speech, you can watch TED talks and read communication books for insights, but nothing can replace the experience of standing in front of an audience and giving a talk. You learn the most when you live it yourself.

Teach what you learn — One of the quickest ways to solidify your understanding of a topic is to teach someone else about it. By articulating concepts in your own unique way, you are solidifying your understanding and uncovering holes in that understanding. Teaching forces you to think about information in a more ordered way and to structure it logically.

If you've ever had to train a new hire or explain a process to a coworker, you probably noticed that trying to put concepts into words clarifies your own understanding. If you don't have someone to teach, still explain what you've learned to yourself, film a short video or write a summary.

Seek Feedback and Iterate – Learning is not only about absorption; it is also about the process of improving with feedback. To hone in on this aspect, seek constructive criticism from your mentors, peers, or supervisors. The best learners don't run from feedback; they run into it and make adjustments over time.

Develop a Habit of Reflection – Spend time to reflect after a task is accomplished or something new is learned. Ask yourself: What worked? What didn't? What do I wish I had done differently so I learn for the next time? Reflection is the tool that turns an experience into education. Noting down some of the stuff that you have learned or writing a learning journal can help you remember it more and make sure you apply it next time you encounter a similar situation.

For example, after giving a presentation you may replay how confident you felt and if you hit your points; or, how you can improve certain things for your next presentation. Mastery is built by incremental improvements.

CURIOSITY AS A COMPONENT OF LEARNING

Curiosity is the fuel for lifelong learning. You become a seeker of knowledge and explore concepts in a deeper manner than you would otherwise. The best professionals and leaders credit a large part of their success to an unquenchable curiosity.

Asking deeper questions is one way to develop curiosity. Instead of mindlessly accepting information, challenge yourself to consider "why" something is that way, and "how" it works. Curiosity drives you to learn more deeply and with more purpose.

Curious people are also better problem-solvers. They don't see challenges as obstacles; they see them as puzzles to solve. It promotes a growth mindset, with an ability to think outside of the box and come up with creative ideas and solutions.

The Science of Memory and Retention

You don't just learn by gathering information — you learn by keeping it and using it. Learning more effectively and being able to access that learning when needed starts with understanding how memory works.

For this reason, one of the best ways you can improve retention is with spaced repetition — a technique that involves reviewing material repeatedly, but at durations that gradually increase over time. Research shows that going over information at certain intervals strengthens neural pathways, making it easier to remember later.

Another highly effective strategy is active recall, in which you attempt to access information from memory instead of passively rereading material. For instance, if you're learning a new idea, see if you can summarize it from memory. This requires your brain to recall the information, strengthening long-term memory.

Why Physical Health Is Linked to Learning?

Most people forget that physical health also plays a huge role in cognitive function. Research has demonstrated that exercise, nutrition, and sleep are all vital for learning and memory.

Regular physical exercise boosts heart rate and strengthens blood flow to the brain, as well as stimulates the release of neuroprotective molecules and aid the growth of new neurons. Even just a walk can increase creativity and problem-solving skills.

Food is related to learning as well. Eating a healthy diet with omega-3 fatty acids, antioxidants, and vitamins are good for the health of your brain. Salmon, blueberries, and nuts, for example, are particularly good for cognitive function.

Probably the biggest factor is sleep, when memory consolidation occurs. The brain uses sleep to process, consolidate and organize information learned throughout the day. Sleeping less undermines concentration, hampers decision-making, and dulls memory retention. Rest is a small but important step to take to improve learning.

USING TECHNOLOGY AS A LEARNING TOOL

Technology has changed the way we learn. Unlike any other time in history, the internet has opened the floodgates for learning through online courses, podcasts, and digital resources. But with a flood of information at our fingertips, it's critical to engage with technology strategically.

While learning through technology, remember to curate quality sourcing. Not all information online is evidence, so you must learn to research well. Following industry experts, enrolling in structured courses, and engaging with reputable publications can ensure you are learning from credible resources.

Moreover, using digital tools like note-taking applications, mind-mapping software, and online educational platforms can assist facilitate and strengthen understanding. Intentionality is the key with technology—use technology to make learning better, not just as distraction.

WHY EMOTIONAL INTELLIGENCE MATTERS IN LEARNING

Soft skills like emotional intelligence (EQ) are also critical to learning. Emotional Intelligence includes self-awareness, empathy, and social and relationship skills that dictate how we process information and interact with those around us in learning environments.

Having an openness to feedback, handling frustration when working with a new topic, and remaining positive about a challenge are all aspects of emotional intelligence that go into how successfully someone learns. Furthermore, good interpersonal skills support collaborative learning environments.

THE NEED FOR ACTIVE LISTENING

Being a good questioner is part of the process of learning, but the other half has to do with your ability to listen. Far too many people listen in order to respond instead of through the lens of seeking to understand. Active listening enables you to absorb the information better, invite more informed follow-up questions, and create better relationships.

By paying close attention, you are able to take in information more effectively and observe details that others might miss. Active listening is being in the moment during a conversation, not letting anything distract you from what the speaker is saying. The best learners are also great listeners since they pick up more knowledge from their environment.

One helpful technique: You can practice reflective listening, in which you paraphrase what you heard someone say to confirm that you understood them correctly. If a colleague is explaining a complex concept, you can reply with, "So what you're saying is …" and repeat the gist of what they just said. This also re-iterates the information for both parties.

EMBRACING LIFELONG LEARNING

Learning does not stop after school or formal training. The top professionals develop a habit of lifelong learning. Keep your curiosity alive, meaning, read trends in your industry, keep up with workshops and continuously seek out ways to become better. Commitment to lifelong learning is a safeguard to falling behind.

Lifelong learners are flexible in their learning. They keep updated on industry changes, embrace new challenges, and actively pursue knowledge. They also know that learning extends beyond the classroom — it unfolds in daily interactions and sharing experiences and taking on new spaces that are uncomfortable.

Developing a lifelong learning habit does not necessarily imply continuously signing up for courses or reading books. It means keeping an open mind, being engaged with new ideas and being open to growing at every stage of your career. What makes a difference is that you keep learning.

Whether you are starting out or well into your career, fast and efficient learning will set you apart. The ones who get ahead aren't necessarily the ones who know the most in the moment — it's the ones who are always open to learning more. Make learning a habit, and you'll always be ready for new challenges and opportunities.

CHAPTER 2:

No Job Is Beneath You

Recognizing the Worth of Each Task

One thing many business owners get wrong is thinking some things are below them. They think that once they reach high enough heights in their careers, they will only need to think about high-level responsibilities. However, the fact is, most high achievers know that no jobs are beneath them. They realize that every task, no matter how small, is a contribution to the bigger picture.

Think of some of the most successful business leaders — many began in entry-level jobs, doing work that others might deem inconsequential. Before Amazon Jeff Bezos was flipping burgers at McDonalds, learning the efficiencies in their process. Elon Musk washed boilers in a lumber mill, before launching many companies' worth Billions. Working in these entry-level roles instilled within them strong work ethic, attention to detail and an understanding of how to begin from the ground up.

Another prime example is Indra Nooyi, former CEO of PepsiCo. She started out as a receptionist during graduate school, working the phones to finance her tuition. Instead of feeling superior to the position, she seized it as a chance to cultivate communication skills and the ability to work under pressure. The lessons she learned from those early years carried over into her management of one of the largest corporations in the world.

By bringing the same sense of pride to all of your responsibilities you show humility, work ethic, and a team player mentality. Developing these principles will put you ahead of the curve in any work environment, leading to bigger opportunities.

Cultivating a Good Work Ethic

A strong work ethic may be the most underrated aspect to finding career success. The people who have it blow many of their peers out of the water, not because they're better or brighter but because they put in the time, have a good attitude, and make a point of taking pride in every part of their job. Building a good work ethic means striving for excellence in respect to everything you do, whether it be a high-stakes presentation or file organization.

A good work ethic involves more than just hard work — it involves working smart. It means making your approach to every task focused, efficient and a commitment to quality performance. When people define hard work most think of it as long hours, but in reality hard work is being consistent, reliable and taking ownership of your tasks. Its consistently following through and delivering results, even when no one is watching.

Humility, And The Role It Plays In Your Career

It may be the most powerful attribute a professional can have, yet many people mistake it for weakness. Your mindset of learning new skills and knowledge is also nurtured by the belief that there is no work below your dignity. You start becoming more flexible, willing to try new things, and able to appreciate the contributions of others.

Let humility encourage you to learn from colleagues at all levels, not just those senior in status. It contributes to building stronger relationships as people like when someone would go the extra mile for the team. It also makes you more personable, which translates to more opportunities to be mentored and to network with colleagues.

I give you the example of Howard Schultz, the former CEO of Starbucks, exemplifying this practice. Schultz, who by his own account had humble beginnings, never forgot that his company's success relied on the importance of every single role in it. As chief Executive, he would visit Starbucks stores daily, talking with baristas and making drinks to stay connected to the daily operations of the business. Not only did this keep him grounded but it also bolstered employee morale.

APPRECIATION FOR THE SMALL THINGS

Most people think that it is only employees working on significant projects or who make big decisions that get noticed by leaders. In actuality leaders remember those who get the little things right. Trust goes to those who are reliable, take ownership of even minor tasks, and consistently perform at a high level. Building trust is one of the fastest ways to level up your career.

Most great leaders put people through tests — with small things to see how they are handled. Only if you can trust someone with the little things will you trust them with bigger things. It's not about doing the work of others — it's about showing that you take every aspect of your job seriously and have the discipline to follow through.

Overcoming the "That's Not My Job" Mentality

One of the most corrosive mindsets in any workplace is the idea that some work is beneath your title. When you become the kind of person who says, "That's not my job," you limit your growth potential.

You should work to shift your mentally to think in terms of contribution instead. Ask yourself, how can I provide value in this situation? And even if a task isn't strictly your responsibility, lending a hand when needed demonstrates initiative. Another benefit is that it lets you learn new skills, cultivate goodwill among your peers and establish a reputation as someone reliable and solutions-oriented.

How the Small Things Open You Up for Big Opportunities

There are endless stories about professionals who began with menial jobs, and then through their hard work and approach earned better opportunities. An experienced receptionist who shows interest in learning more about the business can later work into management. Interns willing to dig deeper in research can earn the trust of executives. An employee who raises his or her hand to take on additional projects can very quickly be seen as a key contributor.

Each job you do well reinforces your credibility. It constructs trust between you, your peers, and your leadership. When others realize you care for the small things with a strong conviction, they will trust you with larger things.

Psychological Benefit of Embracing All of It.

The psychological side of taking pride in all areas of your work — a well-run home or a clean workspace or a well-balanced diet — enhances and improves your career. Research indicates that those who commit themselves to their work, regardless of how insignificant the task, are more satisfied with their jobs. Instead of feeling resentful about certain responsibilities, they are empowered to feel like they put meaningful effort towards something bigger than themselves.

When you accept work instead of fighting the work, it generates a positive feedback loop. You build a reputation for reliability and diligence, which results in more respect from colleagues and supervisors. These small acts of excellence compound over time into bigger career opportunities.

REAL EXAMPLES FOR ADOPTING THIS MINDSET IN YOUR CAREER

If you want to take this mindset on, begin by changing how you approach day to day work. When you do need to re-engage, approach it with a service mentality—stop asking what you have to do and start asking how you can support others. This is the most beneficial mindset — Focusing on being a contributor makes you more valuable to your team and your organization. Another key is taking initiative. Don't wait for instructions, search for opportunities where you can provide value. Reach out to your manager or coworkers, and offer to help out where you can, particularly during busy periods.

THE POWER OF CONTRIBUTION

In any career, not shying away from small tasks, but shining through them, is the way to success. When you tackle each job with passion and pride, you set yourself up for success. You demonstrate that you are reliable, flexible, and willing to go to extra lengths to make sure the work of your organization succeeds.

Not believing in the concept of "beneath you work" to lay the groundwork for long-term career advancement. You earn a reputation as reliable, humble, and dedicated to excellence. And ultimately, this mentality will give you access to places and opportunities that those who shun the little things will never experience.

Final Thought

If you're frustrated with the monotonies of your day, remind yourself: Some of the most successful people in the world did similar work at one point. It's in how they approach it that sets apart those who advance and those who stay stagnant. No job is too small to start out with — it's preparation for something greater.

CHAPTER 3:

BE THE BEST IN YOUR CURRENT ROLE

BE EXCEPTIONAL AT WHAT YOU DO NOW

Many professionals are convinced that the key to career success is in always searching for the next big opportunity. Ambition is important, however, real success is about delivering in your current role. In fact, by being the best at what you do today, you are setting up a really strong base for what you can do next. Those who have demonstrated that they are capable of handling their current roles with excellence attract promotions, new opportunities, and leadership positions.

To be the best in your job, it doesn't mean you do your job right; it means how to do it better. It's the people who do more than they have to that get noticed by the bosses, their coworkers and even clients. They add value in ways beyond their job descriptions, making themselves an indispensable member of the team.

Mastering the Fundamentals

Every profession has core skills that anyone can use to be successful. In mastering the basic competencies that your work demands, you separate yourself from the pack, regardless of whether you're involved in sales, marketing, engineering, healthcare or anything else. The best don't just learn the basics — they refine and iterate them again and again.

Consider professional sports players. The best players in every sport constantly practice the basics. They spend hours repeating simple movements, honing their techniques, making certain that they are perfect in execution. The same principle carries through every path in life — mastery leads to excellence.

To ensure that you keep on improving, make learning part of your daily routine. Consume articles specific to the subject matter, enroll in courses and workshops, and work towards finding mentors to help guide you along the way. Each little step you take toward honing your fundamentals builds up over time to put you on the path to mastering your field.

Building a Reputation for Consistency

One of the most under appreciated yet most powerful qualities in any workplace is reliability. You become someone people want to work with when your boss, colleagues and clients know they can count on you. This involves honoring deadlines, being true to your word and providing consistent results.

Reliability is more than merely being on time; it's following through on promises, paying attention to detail and displaying a level of professionalism that others can depend on.

To be regarded as dependable, be clear in your communications and be proactive. If you think you may not be able to meet a deadline, let your manager know as soon as possible, along with how the deadline could be met. If you say you are going to help a colleague, do so without anyone needing to ask you again. Such small habits help them trust you while also making you more dependable.

CONTINUOUS IMPROVEMENT

The enemy of greatness is complacency. The best professionals always look for improvement, knowledge, and refining their skills. Even if you are already crushing it in your position, there is always something to improve.

The best way to improve is by getting feedback. Inputs from your managers, co-workers, as well as customers (constructive criticism) will surely provide you with valuable insights to strengthen your skills. Consider feedback not as criticism but as a chance to grow.

Regular self-assessments is also a great strategy for continuous improvement. Ask yourself:

- What kind of tasks do I perform well?
- What am I struggling with, and how can I do better?
- What skills can I learn to become more valuable?
- How can I provide more value in my work?

Because you are constantly measuring how you do and fine-tuning, you will always be improving.

Value Beyond Your Job Description

Excelling in your role isn't just about executing assignments; it's about discovering ways to be of value to your organization. This might involve identifying inefficiencies and proposing ways to streamline, mentoring junior employees or taking the initiative on projects that fall outside of your primary role.

Discerning how to add value is not merely about working more hours or taking on more tasks—the key is working differently and contributing meaningfully. New opportunities and promotions are reserved for those that consistently add value.

If there is some process in your company that seems more inefficient than you'd like, make it your mission to offer a solution. When you encounter a colleague who is struggling with a task that you are good at, offer advice. These small contributions demonstrate leadership potential and position you as an integral part of your organization's success.

Staying Engaged and Proactive

Don't find yourself falling into the trap of doing the bare minimum. Many professionals if they don't think they're in their final career landing spot succumb to this. But disengagement can put a stop on your career advancement. Rather than seeing your job merely as a stepping stone, see it as an opportunity to develop skillsets, create relationships and demonstrate your potential.

Such an attitude involves anticipating issues before they appear, taking action without the need to be asked, and showing a sincere interest in providing value in your work. Companies notice employees who take ownership of their role with little supervision, as do leaders.

Staying motivated can be difficult, so to remain engaged set goals around your work space or how you do your work. For instance:

- Set a 30-day challenge to increase your efficiency in one task by 10%.
- Learn a new skill that can be useful for future job objectives.
- Work on a cross departmental project to improve relationships with coworkers.

When you define little and tangible goals, you are motivated with the fact of knowing to what you should strive so that you keep doing your best to get things done.

Foundational Elements that Shape Emotional Intelligence

Technical skills and industry knowledge are essential, but it's the emotional intelligence (EQ) that can take you further in the workplace. High-EQ professionals tend to be great communicators, team players, conflict-resolvers, and leaders. They know how to navigate complexities in the workplace and get along with coworkers and customers alike.

Emotional intelligence consists of self-awareness, empathy and the capacity to regulate emotions during high-stress situations. Not only do those who master these skills do better in their existing roles but they are also well positioned for leadership opportunities.

Using Your Current Role For Your Next Steps

GET ONE-ON-ONE GUIDANCE: The majority of employees start believing that excelling in their role means they must remain there forever. But being the best at your job gets you ready for your next career step. Leaders do look for individuals who can take on additional responsibilities and the first test is mastery of their current role.

If you want to be in a good position in your career, think long term:

- Cultivate relationships with mentors and other leaders in your organization.
- Maintain an open conversation with your supervisor about your long-term goals.
- Keep ears to the ground for company opportunities and signal interest in moving up when appropriate.

Your present job is just the starting point for bigger and better things. The better you do now, the better the opportunities that will be presented to you.

Create Opportunities For Yourself

It's not just about you being your best at what you do, it's about creating your best opportunities for what's next by using your current situation as a catalyst.

You do not pursue opportunities — you create them through the value you provide. The more value you provide, the more opportunities you will attract. The best way to set yourself up for long-term career success is to excel in your current role, and the habits you establish now will carry with you into any stage of your career.

No matter what industry you're in, what position you're in, or what long-term goals you have, the principle is the same: The best way to prepare for your next opportunity is to own the opportunity you have now.

CHAPTER 4:

DEVELOPING YOUR COMMUNICATION ABILITY

COMMUNICATION IS KEY

Communication is a key soft skill that plays a role in all aspects of your career. A seasoned communicator will be a step ahead of everyone else, whether you're pitching an idea at a meeting, crafting an email, negotiating with clients, or collaborating with colleagues. However, poor communication can have the opposite effect — misunderstandings, missed opportunities, broken workplace relationships.

In all disciplines, the ability to express your thoughts concisely, to listen, and to adapt your written or verbal approach depending on an audience — is a skill that sets you apart. Good communication skills will not only help you deliver your best performance, but also help you become a better leader and professional.

How to Master Your Communicative Ability

There is more to verbal communication than verbalizing words; it is about communicating messages effectively so that they are clear, engaging and persuasive. Good verbal communicators get to know their audience, select their words mindfully and modify their tone and delivery to have the greatest effect.

Speaking clearly is an important aspect of improving verbal communication. Your message should be simple and void of any complex terms that makes it hard to follow and understand. Confident body language is also important — look your contacts in the eye, use hand gestures appropriately, and sit straight to show confidence. Also watch your pacing and tone, speaking at a steady rhythm and varying your voice to an appropriate degree to keep your audience engaged. And last, listen by being engaged, nodding, summarizing topics and asking questions. Regardless of whether you are involved in meetings, presentations, or casual discussion, the ability to express yourself well will significantly improve your credibility and influence.

Growing your verbal communication skills also means finding out how to tailor your speech based on your audience. Changing the level of formality is important because speaking to a room of executive is not the same as speaking to a colleague over a coffee. Adding the ability to "code-switch" between professional, technical, and casual tones will make you a better communicator in different contexts. Finally, practicing your articulation and enunciation makes your speech clearer, allowing what you are saying to be interpreted exactly as you intended.

|

The Power of Active Listening

Most people listen to respond, not to understand. Active listening is where you focus entirely on the person speaking, comprehend what they're saying, and then respond.

To develop your active listening skills, begin by focusing on the speaker— setting aside distractions, making eye contact, and displaying sincere curiosity. Refrain from interjecting, letting the speaker finish their thoughts before you prepare a response. Employ reflective listening by restating what was said for clarification, as in, "So what you are saying is..." Lastly, be sure to ask probing questions that demonstrate you are genuinely ruminating on the conversation. Active listening has been shown to not only keep track of data better, but also to build relationships and show respect for others.

Good listeners also attend to the speaker's emotions and tone, not just their words. Becoming more sensitive to the emotions behind a message can help improve empathy and other interpersonal relationships. This is all the more crucial in leadership roles, where conflict resolution and collaboration are key to creating the kind of workplace that drives high performance.

Improving Your Written Communication Skills

In a professional environment, writing is as impactful as verbal communication. Your professionalism and credibility are reflected in emails, reports, proposals and even text messages.

Write clearly and concisely to make your point, cut out the fluff while still providing enough detail. Grammar and spelling are essential; errors can damage your credibility, so proofreading your work is critical. Also tailor your tone to your audience; a formal message to senior executives should not sound like a casual note to a colleague. A well composed email or report can make a vivid impression in the readers' memory vs. poor writing could result in a negative impression of yourself to the reader.

Advanced written communication includes adapting the messaging across media. Writing a business proposal, for example, involves different skills than writing an interesting post for social media. Knowing how to format your writing for various media will ensure your message remains effective — regardless of where it's delivered.

Nonverbal Communication: Communication Beyond Words

Messages are also received and extended based on nonverbal communication. Body language and facial expressions can often express more than just words on their own.

Even the simplest facial expressions can help improve nonverbal communication, so keep that smile warm and eyebrow up, they can shift everything in a conversation! Keep your body language open, arms crossed can indicate defensiveness, whilst an open posture helps facilitate the flow of the conversation. Subtly mirroring the other person's body language can create an instant bond of rapport and trust, making our communications more effective. Last but not least, be mindful of personal space since respecting boundaries creates comfort in professional interactions. Reading nonverbal cues can unlock your power of influence, persuasion and connection with people.

Practicing throughout the day by using a mirror or recording conversations with friends or family members can help pinpoint ways in which we can improve. Many people are not even aware of the unconscious message they give through their gestures and expressions. Becoming more aware of these signals can significantly change how you are seen in your work and social environment.

Navigating Tough Conversations with Confidence

Difficult conversations happen in every career. Whether it's conflict with a coworker, asking for a raise, or giving constructive feedback, managing these conversations is a vital skill.

You just need to be calm and maintain your cool during tough conversations and have self-control over your emotions and approach them with a problem-solving attitude. Be direct but respectful — communicate your concerns clearly without aggression or dismissiveness. Use "I" statements to communicate how you feel without placing blame; for instance, you could say, "I felt concerned when the deadline was missed because it impacted my work schedule." Try and resolve problems by focusing on the solution vs being blinded by the problem. The ability to lead and solve problems begins with communication, especially in times of high pressure.

Another tough conversation can be engaging in diplomacy. At times, it's not only what is said, but also how it is said. You should be soft, but clear, cushioning your criticisms, but still getting your point across. Role-playing to practice the difficult conversation or scripting key responses in advance can help with confidence in the real conversation.

Storytelling Is a Tool For Effective Communication

People love stories because they form emotional bonds between the storyteller and the audience, which makes them easier to remember.

When using storytelling in the most effective way, always make your story relatable by letting your audience in on common experiences. Be creative and express your thoughts with imagination. Be purpose-driven — the story you share should serve a greater purpose and reinforce a key point or lesson that aligns with your communication objectives. It should be short enough to keep your audience engaged, and it should not be so long as to be boring. Storytelling mastery can make you a more persuasive communicator — whether you are convincing colleagues, influencing a team or giving a speech.

Learning How to Speak in Public

Public speaking can be the most dreaded but most essential hurdle in career development. Confidence in public speaking can take you far, whether you're leading a meeting or delivering a keynote address, effective communication is essential.

If you want to become a better public speaker, do your preparation—if you know the material backwards you will build confidence. Rehearse regularly and practice in front of a mirror, record yourself and play it back, and most importantly, present to a trusted colleague or friend. Get the audience involved with storytelling, questions and jokes to keep their attention. Finally, you can keep anxiety in check by remembering to breathe deeply, picture yourself succeeding, and by concentrating on your content, not your fear. With practice comes confidence and comfort.

Communication: The Superpower of your Career

Communication is a competitive edge in any industry. It enables you to form connections, overcome obstacles, sway choices and progress professionally. Through practice and refinement you can leverage communication as your superpower.

Whether you are in tech, arts, clerical, or any field, good communication sets apart good professionals from great ones. The more you work on developing this skill, the more opportunities you will create for yourself in your career.

CHAPTER 5:

GIVE MORE IN VALUE THAN YOU TAKE IN PAYMENT

THE MINDSET OF VALUE CREATION

No matter the industry, the people that go above and beyond are the ones rewarded in their careers. Although most people do what needs to be done as specified in their job description, the best professionals come to work every day ready to deliver more than what is expected of them. They understand that their value created is tied to their long term success, and that value is not as simple as the amount of tasks they complete.

Giving more than you are paid for doesn't necessarily mean working ridiculous hours for no extra pay. It means you can find better ways to work, become more productive, work with others better, and make a positive difference in your organization without it being a part of the job description. People with this mentality regularly unlock new doors to promotions, leadership, and money. The trick is to move away from transactional work and adopt a philosophy of contribution.

How Value and Compensation Are Related

So many professionals come into their jobs with the mindset that they should only do as much work as their salary covers. But the reality is that compensation follows value, not the reverse. The best end up working at a higher level before they are compensated at that level, and the rest falls into place.

All businesses and organizations are founded on the basis of an exchange of value. Employers hire you because you can give them more skills, efficiencies, creativity, and innovation at work. Those who show that they can deliver value over and above their peers are the ones who receive the accolades, promotions, raises, etc. The trick is being focused on making impact and not just working. The employees who benefit from long-term careers with an organization are those who drive results, enhance efficiency, or drive revenue growth.

How to Add More Value to Your Role

Going above and beyond and anticipating the needs of others is one of the simplest ways to deliver additional value. Proactive employees do not sit and wait for instructions—this means they see the potential areas in which things can be improved and take action. Those who take the initiative to streamline a process, improve a system, or solve a recurring problem are generally recognized for their contributions. Employees who anticipate difficulties and take steps to prepare for them not only show reliability, they show leadership potential. Because initiative generates momentum in a career, it often leads to fresh opportunities.

A key trait of high performers is delivering high quality work. Demonstrating your attention to detail, verifying tasks have been done and ensuring that you go above and beyond to not only meet but exceed expectations establishes trust, credibility and leads to more opportunities to be trusted with bigger, better projects. Good work is recognized as such and professionals who tirelessly demonstrate excellence in their endeavors are deemed invaluable assets to their teams and organizations.

Creating more efficiency and productivity also drives a greater value. Always searching for ways to work smarter instead of harder, enables professionals to achieve high volumes within short time frames without compromising on quality. Learning to manage time well and weed out inefficiencies to keep output at peak performance. Those who learn to optimize workflows or implement new technologies that enhance productivity become assets to their teams.

There is a value you can give that is even greater than just your individual performance which is helping others be successful. Being there for your team, offering your expertise, training juniors, assisting colleagues, and facilitating team efforts leads to team success, and everyone loves an indispensable employee. People who take the time to invest in the growth of their colleagues, build stronger teams, increase morale, and establish themselves as leaders in their organizations. Working together and sharing knowledge improves efficiency and creates a culture of success.

In a dynamic workplace, learning new skills is crucial. Continual learning and consistent evaluation of how to apply your learnings ensures professional growth and increases the value of an employee to their organization. Those who are not stagnant in their career become eager to learn new things, get good at their work, and find their place in the corporate world. The return on investment can vary based on multiple factors, however, learning can better equip a person while helping them grow in skill, confidence and credibility within their professional circles.

Be a problem-solver. It is one thing to remind the world of everything that's wrong; it's a far greater thing to identify what might be done to remedy that wrong. Providing constructive recommendations and an ability to deal with challenges demonstrate investment in the organization's success. Innovation is key for businesses to flourish, meaning that individuals willing to solve problems and make decisions — even when those decisions have a slight chance of success — can amass influence and be exposed to a great amount of career opportunities.

Having a positive attitude is a very important factor too in how the value is perceived. Members of a team who tackle tasks with a passion for the work, the fortitude to withstand adversity and a solution-oriented approach to problem solving make up a powerful workforce that drives company morale and productivity. People who are able to adapt with change or keep moving forward when problems arise and who have their eyes on the future are also the ones who are most often given more responsibility. A positive mindset infuses the team environment with positivity at all levels, enabling the team to see challenges as growth opportunities rather than roadblocks to success.

Why Offering Extra Value Equals Career Advancement

Repeat value-oriented contributors rapidly establish themselves as invaluable trusted members in their teams. Earned trust results in more reliability, better responsibilities, and more authority in the organization. Naturally, opportunities for leadership, raises, and advancement in their careers come to them. The value creators are the ones who get pulled on to the big projects, the profile roles and the industry accolades.

Value creators gain skills and experience at a quicker pace than their minimum-doing peers do. If they continue to reach beyond their job descriptions, they learn, expand their networks, and become viewed as subject matter experts. As time goes on, that extra expertise translates to higher levels of professional and financial success. Employees with proven track records are recruited onto high-stakes initiatives and offered valuable career-building opportunities.

Value creation also means better relationships at work. Those who stand up for and promote their peers consistently develop goodwill within their organizations. A reputation for reliability and excellence leads to mentorship opportunities, senior leadership support, and long-term career stability. Leaders seek people who not only succeed, but who bring up those around them. The better you are at engendering trust and good relations, the more you will be able to increase the future potential of your career.

One of the biggest advantages of staying oriented to value creation is the ability to future-proof your career. Sectors change and labor markets change, but people who make themselves valuable will always find work. Those professionals that are consistently exploring new avenues to innovate, adapt and expand their skill sets are far less susceptible to the ebbs and flows of the job market. They are also more often solicited by employers with job offers and new career paths, allowing them a degree of certainty and control over their professional future.

THE POWER OF OVERDELIVERING

Offering more value than you are paid for is one of the best career hacks to fast track your career success. Those who think this way follow the path to become valued assets in every organization.

When your focus is on over-delivering, being proactive, supporting those around you and constantly being better, you become an above-average professional. When you become someone who always gives more than what is expected of you, compensation, and promotions will automatically follow. The secret: treat your career as a contribution, as such, the more you give, the more you will be rewarded in due time.

Building a career on a foundation of value offering not only yields monetary success but invokes deeper personal satisfaction. When people take pride in the work they do, learn, and enable others to be successful they feel good, have better job satisfaction and have more purpose. Enabling a meaningful difference in the work inspires a meaningful sense of professional accomplishment. People who live by this principle of overdelivering are never short on career opportunities in their lives, they keep going up in their careers.

CHAPTER 6:

GET READY FOR OPPORTUNITIES LONG BEFORE YOU GET THEM

LEVERAGING PREPARATION LEADS TO SUCCESS

Success is rarely accidental. The people who do great things in their careers are the ones who have been preparing for their luck long before it arrives. Most people wait to develop the necessary skills until after a promotion is available, a new job listing appears, or a leadership role opens. The most successful professionals, however, are prepared, getting the knowledge, experience, and frame of mind they need to jump on opportunities well before they come up.

By taking initiative to build skills and establish yourself as a top candidate for promotions, you dramatically improve your odds of getting ahead. People who are prepared for opportunities before they come are not only at an advantage to their peers for those opportunities, but those who prepare in advance have a habit of creating new opportunities as well. People who are constantly learning, growing, and preparing for the next step are noticed by employers and leaders.

BUILDING A GROWTH MINDSET

Your future starts with a growth mindset, the understanding that intelligence and skills can be improved with effort and hard work. Growth mindset professionals view every action not as a sequence of random events, but a series of opportunities to learn and grow.

Taking ownership of your own career development means thinking about what skills and knowledge you will need to thrive in future roles and developing them now. Whether that is through getting more training, reading about top professionals, getting experience with mentors, or trying other challenges that are out of your comfort zone. More importantly, those who are always looking to better themselves will be the ones who are well-positioned to take on more responsibility when the opportunity arises.

INVESTING IN CONTINUOUS LEARNING AND SKILL DEVELOPMENT

Continuous learning is one of the best ways to prepare ourselves for success in the opportunities ahead. The work environment is ever-changing, and those who don't change with it will be left behind. It is the professionals who pursue knowledge, and enhance their set of skill that find the most success.

Lifelong learning does not need to be formal education. This can be everything from self-study to attending conferences and various professional development programs, to on-the-job learning. Be it refining leadership qualities, mastering a new technology or sharpening communication skills, each skill acquired today is an asset to take advantage of opportunities tomorrow.

Build a Network Before You Need It

Most people only start networking when they are looking for a new job or opportunity. But the best networks are constructed long before they are necessary. Strong connections with coworkers, mentors, professionals in the field, and thought leaders form a network of support that can lead to new opportunities.

To build a professional network, you need to interact with people regularly and in a meaningful manner. That might mean networking at industry events, participating in conversations on industry forums, helping out colleagues, or connecting with former coworkers. An established network enhances visibility, provides perspective on career paths, and often results in unexpected opportunities.

A good networker also has a reputation synonymous with value. When you help other people succeed—be it by providing mentorship, referrals, or collaborating on projects—you reinforce your professional ties. With time, these connections can lead to career-defining opportunities.

Show Them You're Ready

One of the best ways to set yourself up for future opportunities is to excel in your present role. Some people, unfortunately, think they'll suddenly start working at a higher level once a promotion or new position opens up. But usually the people who get promoted the fastest are the ones already operating at the next level before they get the title.

Exhibiting leadership qualities, taking the initiative, and consistently doing great work communicates to others who make the decisions that you are prepared for more. People who go above and beyond in their roles, owners of their responsibilities, and all-around positive people are noticed by those in leadership. If you establish yourself as a person who takes on bigger tasks, you are more likely to be chosen to be promoted.

Exceeding expectations at work doesn't have to involve laboring longer hours. It means making a bigger impact — by streamlining processes, helping others succeed or finding new examples of how to help meet company targets. Proactively improving your work environment shows that you are ready for more responsibility.

BUILDING STRONG DECISION-MAKING AND PROBLEM-SOLVING ABILITIES

Future roles are usually accompanied with added responsibilities, which means you will need to make some tough decisions and will have some complex problems to solve. Strengthening decision-making and problem-solving skills beforehand equips leaders for high-stakes scenarios before they happen.

By practicing critical thinking, looking at the problem from all angles, adapting and learning from your mistakes, our ability to solve problems improves. Pursuing strategic thinking challenges and projects also offers significant preparation for more rigorous positions later on.

Decision-making is also learning about how to balance risk and reward. People who can analyze these situations rationally, make well-informed decisions, and execute these decisions with conviction, are viewed as capable leaders. Cultivating these skills in smaller, lower risk day-to-day situations primes you for the bigger challenges ahead in your career.

Flexibility and Adaptability

Inaction is the enemy of change, and inaction is the enemy of career growth. As long as you are flexible, there are things to learn, and new opportunities to explore. Change can be chaotic, but those who learn to navigate chaos can not only survive, but typically thrive because others became lost and look to the navigators for guidance. Many forget that it is not the strongest or wisest that succeed it is the most adaptable.

Learning to be adaptable requires embracing the unknown and seeing change as a chance to develop instead of a risk. The more you adapt, the more ready you will be to identify and take advantage of opportunities as they come.

Adaptability also demands resilience. Setbacks and challenges are part of any career path, but what separates successful people from others is the ability to learn from experience and an openness to change. To be relevant in the job market that is ever-evolving, a flexible and adaptive mindset is essential. You must be willing to improve yourself constantly and prepare for uncertainty.

Positioning is Key

Preparation is more than skills acquisition — it's about strategic positioning. That means having a good professional reputation, connecting with decision-makers, and making sure your work and accomplishments are on the radar of those who matter. Those who keep meticulous records of their successes, update their resumes and portfolios regularly, and communicate their value effectively tend to be on the radar when new opportunities arise.

Maintaining a record of your achievements and contributions—be it a professional journal, updated LinkedIn profile or personal portfolio—means you'll always be ready to sell your services. And when opportunities arise, knowing how to articulate your past successes and demonstrate your readiness can be the difference between being ready or simply waiting your turn.

Fortune Favors the Prepared

I dare say that the best opportunities do not fall to those who are merely waiting for them, but rather to those who have been preparing for it from the start. Achieving success comes from hard work, dedication, and planning. By taking a proactive stance toward career growth and acquiring the necessary skill set, while always having a readiness frame of mind, you prepare yourself so that once the right opportunity comes along, you are more than ready to make it happen.

Those people who take the initiative to invest in themselves will find doors opening — and opening easier — for this reason. The unprepared will see much fewer opportunity and be left wondering why. The important thing is that you prepare now, so when opportunity strikes, you are ready to rise to the occasion.

This highly competitive knowledge economy has made a career based on preparation a must for those who are looking to capitalize on the greatest amount of opportunity. Those who actively look to improve their skills, build networks, and seek continual improvement will always have a job. Approaching preparation as a long-term investment positions you not just to succeed but also to adapt to an ever-evolving professional landscape.

CHAPTER 7:

DO WHAT YOU SAY

KEEPING YOUR WORD AND ITS SIGNIFICANCE IN CAREER GROWTH

Reliability is one of the most important traits a person can offer in the professional world. People who fulfill their promises become trustworthy, foster relationships, and open doors for career growth. Your word is a promise, when you do what you say you're going to do people see you as reliable, responsible, and trustworthy. On the flip side, breaking promises can tarnish your image and restrict your path in the future as well.

Following through on your commitments isn't just about integrity — it's also about professionalism and accountability. Nothing will kill your credibility more in a team collaboration culture faster than failing to follow through on tasks or meeting expectations. If it's delivering on promises met, or meeting them on time, or being available for someone in need, honoring commitments lays down the groundwork for long sustained success.

The Worth of Trust: How to Keep Commitments

Trust is the foundation of all professional relationships. Your peers, clients and leaders need to know they can count on you. Your integrity is ingrained in everything you do. When people see you as someone who consistently delivers on what you say, they look for your input, give you critical projects, recommend you for leading positions.

In contrast, consistently failing to follow through can have the opposite effect. When a person always fails to meet deadlines, cancel meetings or not deliver on their commitments, it creates frustration and a lack of trust in their competence. Long-term, this can lead to missed opportunities and a black mark on your name.

Exemplifying this each and every day is crucial to your success. Trust is not developed overnight, but rather through small and large interactions overtime time. Reliability is the outcome of being on time, meeting deadlines, and producing work that is of high quality. Trust breeds strong professional relationships, synergize collaboration flows, and new career paths open up organically.

The Relationship Between Accountability and Development

If you really want to shine in your career, one of the best ways to do so is by being responsible for your commitments and actions. This means owning your responsibilities, being honest when things go wrong and working on solution to overcome issues. Taking responsibility is a sign of good leadership, and it gives people confidence in you.

Those who take ownership of their work are often handed bigger responsibilities. Managers and executives prefer employees that can be counted on to complete vital projects with minimal supervision. When you hold yourself accountable, it shows that you can be trusted to be proactive and drive results, and that often leads to promotions.

Being accountable means no excuses. DON'T play the blame game: Real professionals don't cover their backs when they screw up, they look for solutions and strive to be better. An accountability-based workplace culture embrace accepting feedback and encouraging employees to take calculated risks to achieve excellence and contribute.

Enhancing Your Commitment and Reliability

Setting the bar as realistically as possible is one of the best processes for making sure you do what you say you will do. Do not overwhelm yourself or imply guarantees that you cannot deliver on! You are better off under promising and over delivering than to promise the world and deliver nothing, be honest about what is possible. Not only do you stay credible, but it avoids a lot of needless strain.

Improving time management is another important strategy. Being reliable takes great organizational skills and the ability to prioritize. Time management tools such as calendars, task lists and project management systems can help you keep track of all of your commitments and ensure you meet those deadlines. If you organize your time well, you are sure to keep to your promises and actually create consistency in your work.

It's also important to communicate clearly when you are maintaining commitments. In the event that things change and you can't follow through with an obligation, let people know that as soon as you can. Proposing alternative solutions or renegotiating deadlines is a sign of responsibility and respect for others' time. People value honesty and proactive problem-solving over excuses.

Discipline will help you to stay on track and continue pursuing the goal, even when motivation is lower. Those at the top of their fields build habits that support reliability—including creating tentative schedules in advance, giving themselves due dates, and having accountability measures to ensure they are doing what they said they would do.

How Commitment Affects Workplace Culture

If you can foster an environment of commitment and trust, team members will start to depend on each other, productivity rises, and projects flow more smoothly. When leaders exhibit commitment and deliver on their promises, they establish what becomes an organization's culture.

On the other hand, lack of commitment breeds inefficiency, missed opportunities and conflict in the workplace. When employees fail to deliver on their end, it adds more burden to others and builds frustration among groups. A strong value-based culture around accountability is essential to ensuring everyone is doing their part to contribute the organizations overall success.

Commitment also boosts morale at the office. When employees trust that their coworkers will deliver on promises, they are more engaged and motivated. Organizations guided by a culture of commitment promote a collaborative team-spirit, decrease unnecessary levels of toxic stress, and realize their goals more efficiently.

Walking the Walk: Importance of Commitment as a Leader

The bottom line is that the best leaders know that commitment is essential, so it is something that they pay attention to in their professional behavior. An environment that promotes keeping promises starts with having exemplary leadership, a source of inspiration for your team who would conduct themselves accordingly. Employees turn to their leaders for guidance, and when leaders model accountability, others are inspired to do the same.

Showing transparency and honesty about challenges is one of the best ways to lead by example. When leaders acknowledge their own mistakes, take ownership of setbacks, and push toward solutions, they cultivate an environment where accountability is the norm. And this, in turn, enhances team cohesion and trust.

Leaders know that commitments go beyond just getting things done. They dedicate themselves to their teams, their own professional development, and making their offices a great place to be. Leaders who are reliable and involved, build loyalty and inspire ambition in their staff.

The other component of commitment as a leader is consistency. Constantly changing priorities or failing to follow through on commitments leads to uncertainty within teams. Good leaders do what they say, provide clarity on expectations, and back up their words with actions.

THE LASTING REWARDS OF FOLLOWING THROUGH ON COMMITMENTS

If you do what you say you are going to do on a consistent basis, you will quickly develop a reputation that will follow you throughout your career. Your dependability becomes a hallmark of your reputation, making you an attractive candidate for promotions, leadership assignments, and new job opportunities. People prefer working with those that they trust, and trust is built through being consistent.

If you establish yourself as the kind of person who shows up and delivers, chances are good that you'll find yourself receiving referrals, recommendations, and endorsements for other career opportunities. This can be particularly helpful in fields where reputation and networking are key to career progression. Long-term success is built on a track record of reliability.

Reliability: A Career Superpower

Following through on commitments is one of the most basic tenets for long-term career success. When individuals consistently do what they say they will do, they build trust, earn respect, and create opportunities for growth. Realistic expectations are essential to manage time and set the right expectations because overpromising and underdelivering are the attributes of somebody who is not trustworthy; to build trust, one needs to be seen as the person who delivers only what he/she can do and does it on time. Your manner of communication is also crucial, as you need to communicate transparently without mincing words and without sugar-coating. Setting a few rules for self-discipline will go a long way in ensuring you are seen as someone who can be trusted.

Reliability not only means to be on time — reliability means you are honest, professional and responsible. Those who follow through on their commitments will stand out at work and prepare themselves for leadership and advancement. In a world where trust is a big part of human capital, one of the most impactful ways to ensure sustained career success is to be someone who does what they say they'll do.

The key behind success is not talent or intelligence, it is consistency. Those who consistently deliver results over and over again build the confidence of others around them. Trustworthiness leads to opportunities, builds strong professional networks, and lays the foundation for lasting success. When you incorporate commitment and accountability as the foundations of your career, you set yourself up for ongoing success and fulfillment.

CHAPTER 8:

COLLABORATING WITH PEOPLE WHO ARE DIFFERENT FROM YOU

WHY YOU SHOULD EMBRACE DIVERSITY OF PERSPECTIVE IN YOUR ORGANIZATION

Understanding how to work with people who think differently than you is essential for any career. Getting educated on how to handle diverse perspectives is crucial in developing a sense of empathy for the groups involved. In general, every team member has a different background, experience, personality, and approaches to problem-solving, and learning to deal with different perspectives helps teams grow, stimulate innovation, and ultimately contribute to both personal and professional growth.

Diversity of thought is no longer just a buzzword in today's workplace — it's mandatory. Companies and organizations that create a culture that values and supports diverse perspectives generally outperform those that do not. Being able to navigate these differences and appreciate them helps professionals become more flexible, build better relationships, and provide important contributions to their teams.

The best companies have made it a point to hear from people who have different expertise and backgrounds. While differences in opinion may lead to friction at times, they are an incredible fuel for making better decisions. Thanks to diverse teams, assumptions are challenged and ideas tested, resulting in better strategies and ultimately innovation.

Navigating the Challenge of Different Perspectives

Diversity in thought certainly has its merits, but it can be a double edged sword too. We tend to be drawn to those who have similar thoughts to our own, as clear communication and collaboration is much simpler when our views align. Although collaborating with people who possess different views are an occasional source of misunderstanding, disagreement and frustration, they often lead to stronger outcomes.

These challenges are overcome through self-awareness, emotional intelligence, and active listening. Hearing others out, knowing that other people may feel differently, not insisting that someone else's opinion on a given topic is wrong, just different. When team members choose to prioritize shared purpose over personal agendas, potential conflicts serve as opportunities for increased understanding and improved problem resolution.

This is also about separating the professional from the personal. This can provoke emotions when we see it from a different perspective. Learning how to disagree constructively, without getting personal, is a critical professional skill.

The Importance of Active Listening in Collaboration

Practice active listening is one of the most impactful strategies you can leverage when collaborating with people who are different than you. That means not only listening but listening fully and not just waiting to respond. It is all about asking clarifying questions, rephrasing important ideas and showing that you are listening and value the other person's point of view.

Active listening also builds rapport and fosters understanding to ensure that everyone feels like a valued team member. It also minimizes misinterpretation and enables teams to reach consensus faster. When people feel heard, they contribute more freely and move towards common goals with a sense of collaboration.

Incorporating others' points of view, even if they strongly differ from your own, shows respect and willingness to listen. Which creates an environment where co-workers can share ideas without fear of rejection or judgment. Active listening skills go a long way in improving collaboration with others and making you a better leader: A crucial part of a successful leader is working with many different perspectives on a daily basis.

Different People Communicate Differently

We all process information and communicate differently. Some people like a direct, to-the-point, "just get to it" kind of conversation, while others need more context and background information before reaching conclusions. Adapt your communication, because if you can understand and adjust your style to fit with the people you are doing business with, you can really get things done faster and easier.

When dealing with analytical thinkers, focus on data, logic, clear reasoning. Creative thinkers respond more to the story, the vision, and the abstract. Awareness of these differences and your ability to adapt will result in better relationships and higher performance within teams.

Flexibility in terms of communication style is especially critical in leadership and client-facing roles. A well-informed communicator knows how to tailor their voice, tempo, and style according to the listeners. This provides professionals with the opportunity to adjust their communication style, depending on how colleagues and clients respond to different strategies, to create more meaningful connections.

Strength in Differences

Instead of seeing other perspectives as barriers, professionals should see differing opinions as paths for growth. If teams bring together various viewpoints, they can see greater creativity in the solutions they find. Rather than relying on a single dominant insight, organizations gain multi-faceted thoughts and opinions to solve problems.

This means creating an environment that empowers all team members to speak up and share their opinions in order to capture different ideas possibly leading to stronger solutions. This technique allows teams to leverage the diversity of their backgrounds and experiences to their fullest.

Professionals should also be intentional about seeking outside perspectives. Promoting innovation through cross-functional collaboration, or by networking with colleagues from other departments, industries, or cultures, people can gain perspectives that enrich their problem-solving approach. More exposure gives you diverse ways of thinking to challenge assumptions and make you adaptable.

How to Navigate Conflicts in a Constructive Way

Working with people who think differently can lead to disagreements — that is inevitable — but how these disagreements are handled is what creates even greater roadblocks or stepping stones. Rather than avoiding conflicts or going on the defensive like many professionals, approach disagreements with a sense of curiosity and an open mind.

Resolving conflict constructively means you put the issue above your differences. It calls for professionals to stay calm, listen actively and look for solutions that serve the team's greater goals. Well managed conflict is also associated with stronger relationships, improved decision-making, and greater creativity in teams.

Viewing conflicts as opportunities for growth contribute positively towards long term professional development. Instead of making disagreements personal, view them as opportunities to hone ideas and build greater understanding. Teams that learn to engage conflicts in a constructive way create a setting for critical thinking and innovation.

Learning from Others

Every person you interact with has something important to teach you. You get to learn a new way of thinking, a different culture, and potentially a new way of solving problems — being open to learning from others broadens your worldview and brings new skills for you to add to your toolkit. The most successful professionals actively seek out multiple perspectives, ask probing questions, accept feedback and remain receptive to new concepts.

People who have diversity of thinking in their environment tend to be more rounded while working with their tasks. Embracing different perspectives fosters adaptability and positions professionals for leadership roles, where the capacity to navigate through complexity and align diverse teams is paramount.

It helps to also look for mentorship from people with external viewpoints. Hear from leaders with special backgrounds or a specific area of expertise, who provide insights that push you out of your standard way of thinking. Access to diverse mentors allows for continuous learning beyond your immediate circle.

THE NEED FOR DIVERSE THINKING

Diversity is not merely a term in the workplace, and working with people of different ways of thinking is not just about collaboration, it is also about achieving more. Understanding how to work well with people with diverse backgrounds, experiences and points of view is a critical skill in the modern workplace.

By using active listening, embracing differences, and handling discrepancies positively, professionals can channel differences into strengths. Diversity of thought fuels innovation, enables diverse teams, and propels your own career forward. The best leaders who learn to navigate through various perspectives will find themselves leading, influencing and thriving in any professional ecosystem.

The best professionals and institutions recognize that it is at the intersection of ideas that we truly make leaps toward progress. Embracing diverse points of view leads to more creativity, better decisions, and greater working together. In an era where many prefer to stay in their cognitive bubble and cling to their points of view, making an effort to learn from others, adapt our communication style, and resolve conflicts wisely, is what stands out and opens us up to greater opportunities.

CHAPTER 9:

BRINGING IT ALL TOGETHER

In this book we have discussed the principles that lead to a successful and fulfilling career. Every chapter was meant to offer you actionable lessons and key insights meant to empower professionals to navigate their career with confidence, adaptability, and excellence. So now as we wrap up it is time to review these lessons and see how they come together to build the foundation of success that can last a lifetime.

MASTERING THE ART OF LEARNING

Learning well is the most genuine fundamental of growth. Those with a thirst for knowledge, a flexible approach to new challenges, and a drive for lifelong learning will find themselves miles ahead of the rest. We need to learn, grow, and change, if we stay stagnant so will our opportunity. By having a growth mindset, using effective learning techniques, and improving our ability to learn, we can become agile professionals in a changing world. None of us are simply "educators"— learning is not restricted to schoolrooms and training facilities; it is something we do every day, taking in knowledge, establishing best guesses, and sharpening our abilities over time.

The most successful at getting things done take personal responsibility for their learning, finding mentors, reading books, going to seminars, and trying out new things. They learn what they need and go learn ahead of when they need it, not after, and they utilize each learning opportunity on their path to long-term goals. When professionals train their mindset for learning, they build a career that is future-proof, adaptable, and essential wherever they are working.

WORK ETHIC AND COMMITMENT

Success does not come by waiting for things to happen; it comes by being ready for opportunity. Professionals take ownership of their work and hold themselves accountable for their actions — whether it's doing well in their job or following through with what they say, creating value and trust is paramount, which ensures that they are an asset to their organization. High achievers are also people who follow through, respect deadlines and keep their word. People who follow through and fulfill their promises become valued professionals and build strong relationships that can lead to valuable opportunities down the line.

For many of those who become successful in their field, it all comes down to their work ethic, which is the differentiating factor between those who achieve success and those who remain stagnant in their careers. However, going the extra mile, showing accountability and initiative stands out and shows commitment and leadership potential. When you are professionals that consistently show up, do the work, and take ownership of your work, you develop a track record of reliability. This track record, in turn, builds credibility — and sets individuals up for promotions and greater responsibilities and leadership roles.

Providing Value And Treating Every Task Like It Matters

One of the biggest sort of switches in mindset that can help you get on in your career is the realization you need to take pride in every task, no matter how small. Providing more value than what you are being paid for keeps the big picture in mind, builds trust, and demonstrates your value. Giving every task the same level of conviction cultivates a solid work ethic, earns a reputation for reliability, and opens opportunities.

Being proud of your work makes you more invested leading to you being more detail-oriented and efficient in it. Leaders and decision-makers observe those who consistently work hard — whether it's drafting an email, making a report, or managing an important initiative.

Moreover, realize that all tasks provide some sort of value. People own their work more and perform at a higher level when they realize that every contribution counts. Not only is this good for the individual in terms of career advancement, this ultimately results in stronger teams and organizations.

Collaboration And Communication: The Pillars Of Influence

No career exists in a vacuum. Collaboration, particularly with those who think differently, fuels innovation, builds teams, and fortifies a culture of respect. Such effective communication — verbal and nonverbal — is the art of knowledge that makes good professionals into great leaders.

People who can hold difficult conversations, negotiate respectfully and value alternative viewpoints are best positioned for success in these multifaceted workplace environments. Collaborative teams are more innovative, as they create a broader range of ideas and pull from different experiences. As a result, professionals who are good in team environments come to be known for their capacity to unite people and propel projects ahead.

Also, leadership opportunities open up through mastering communication skills. Those who communicate a clear vision, instill confidence and listen to the needs of their teams build strong organizational cultures. Professionals can find success at every stage of their career path by continuing to hone communication skills through writing, public speaking, or presenting.

PREPARATION, A DIRECT PATH TO OPPORTUNITY

Things do not come easy — they come from preparedness and foresight. Those who do the best are the ones who learn abilities they require before they actually need to utilize them. Whether you are working on establishing a professional network, enhancing your decision-making skills, or pursuing mentorship, those who take action are better positioned to recognize and capitalize on opportunities when they present themselves.

Professionals who invest in self-development and growth before the opportunity presents itself are better prepared and are more competitive candidates. They are the ones who are recommended for promotions, chosen for leadership programs, and tapped to lead new initiatives.

Constant improvement in their skills as well as awareness of opportunities enables professionals to transition with greater ease. Whether taking on a new job, starting a business or changing industries, one has to prepare ahead of time to ensure a more seamless and successful transition.

Building a Career That Lasts

Long-term success is about being incremental and therefore sustainable. Habits and principles described in this book are not reinforcement, all or nothing strategies, but continual commitments. Learning attitude, work ethic, communication, collaboration and preparation are all key for any career path.

Those who continue to stretch themselves, evolve and let their work reflect their values will find the greatest opportunities. In order to have a career that lasts, its important to have clear goals, stay motivated, and balance your ambition with your well-being. It is those who make a real difference in the lives of others by providing support for their coworkers, and their organizations that will have empowering legacies.

Final thought: Success is a decision

Every career is different, but the principles of career success are fundamentally the same. Anyone who commits to continuous learning, practices integrity, shows gratitude for all work, and invests in the future can create a meaningful and rewarding career. Success is less about waiting for the right moment and more about creating the right moment by doing work consistently and to the best of your abilities.

Your career is the sum total of the choices you make every day. Choose to learn. Choose to work hard. Choose to provide value. Choose to be reliable. Decide to work with one another and communicate well. Prepare for the opportunities before they present themselves. If you follow these guidelines, success will come.

Double down on these lessons, double down on the skill sets, keep pushing the excellence envelope. What you do today determines what tomorrow looks like.

Stay adaptable, welcome challenges, and continue working towards betterment. No matter where you are in your career the values and skills preached in this book should help guide you through each phase of it with confidence and intentionality.